EXTREME SCIENTISTS™

WEATHER WATCHERS: CLIMATE SCIENTISTS

JUDY MONROE PETERSON

PowerKiDS press.

New York

To Jenna, Abbie, Ryan, and Morgan

Published in 2009 by The Rosen Publishing Group, Inc.
29 East 21st Street, New York, NY 10010

First Edition

Editor: Amelie von Zumbusch
Book Design: Kate Laczynski
Photo Researcher: Jessica Gerweck

Photo Credits: Cover, pp. 1, 11, 15, 21 © National Geographic/Getty Images; p. 5 © Aurora/Getty Images; p. 7 © www.istockphoto.com; p. 9 © Jim Reed/Getty Images; p. 13 © Peter Essick/Getty Images; p. 17 Shutterstock.com; p. 19 © AFP/Getty Images.

Library of Congress Cataloging-in-Publication Data

Peterson, Judy Monroe.
    Weather watchers : climate scientists / Judy Monroe Peterson. — 1st ed.
        p. cm. — (Extreme scientists)
    Includes index.
    ISBN 978-1-4042-4527-3 (library binding)
    1. Climatologists—Vocational guidance—Juvenile literature. 2. Meteorologists—Vocational guidance—Juvenile literature. 3. Meteorology—Juvenile literature. I. Title.
    QC869.5.P48 2009
    551.6023—dc22

                                    2008010548

Manufactured in the United States of America

CONTENTS

Studying Climates 4

What Makes Climates Change? 6

Working Together..8

How Do You Measure Weather?.......................10

Stations, Balloons, and Satellites....................12

Working in Labs..14

Learning from the Rocks......................................16

Clues in Ice and Trees...18

Predicting Climate Change 20

An Important Job 22

Glossary 23

Index 24

Web Sites..24

Studying Climates

What kind of climate does the place you live have? Climate is the weather **patterns** in an **area** over a long time. Weather happens every day. On any given day, the weather in a place may be rainy, snowy, hot, or cold. However, if there are many days over many years when it rains, a place can be said to have a rainy climate. One area with a rainy climate is the American Northwest.

Climate scientists study Earth's climate. They learn how climates form and change. Climate scientists also study what weather patterns do to Earth's **surface**. These scientists guess how climates may change in the **future**, too.

In 1995, no plants grew near Antarctica's Palmer Station. In 2004, this scientist found that the climate had changed so much that many small plants were growing there.

What Makes Climates Change?

Natural events can cause climate change. For example, Earth has volcanoes, or places where melted rock from deep inside Earth pours out onto Earth's surface. Big volcanic **eruptions** often let out huge clouds of ash. After an eruption, some ash remains in Earth's **atmosphere**. This ash blocks some of the Sun's rays from reaching Earth and can cool Earth's climate.

People also cause climate change. Around the world, people burn and cut down forests. Forest trees take in a gas called carbon dioxide from the air. Since there are now fewer trees, more carbon dioxide makes its way into Earth's atmosphere. The carbon dioxide traps warmth inside the atmosphere and makes Earth warmer.

Every year, huge numbers of trees in rich, wet forests called rain forests are cut down. This means far more carbon dioxide is now entering Earth's atmosphere.

Working Together

Earth's oceans and atmosphere both play important parts in forming climates. Therefore, the scientists who study each of these areas can be considered climate scientists. Oceanographers study Earth's oceans. Oceans warm up and cool down more slowly than land surfaces. These giant bodies of water help keep Earth's **temperatures** fairly even.

Atmospheric scientists study Earth's atmosphere. For example, they study how winds in the atmosphere move heat and water around Earth. Certain atmospheric scientists, called meteorologists, **predict** what the weather in the near future will be. Meteorologists measure weather conditions, such as temperature, wind, and rainfall, and use these facts to make their predictions.

Some meteorologists study lightning. The scientists study how lightning forms and try to figure out where it is likely to move.

Climate scientists use many tools to take careful measurements of temperature, wind, and water. Special **thermometers**, called electronic thermometers, measure temperature exactly. Weather vanes, also called wind vanes, show wind direction. These tools have moving arrows, which point in the direction from which wind is coming. A tool called an **anemometer** measures wind speed.

Climate scientists use a tool called a **hygrometer** to measure how much water is in the air. They use several tools to study precipitation, or forms of water falling from the sky. For example, scientists measure how much rain falls with a rain gauge. They often use a Boulay board to measure snowfall.

This climate scientist is carefully measuring the seawater and ice in a part of the Arctic Ocean called the Canada Basin.

11

Stations, Balloons, and Satellites

Many climate scientists work in weather stations. About 10,000 weather stations are found across the world. Many stations are on land. Other stations are on ships at sea. Scientists also send special weather balloons high into the air. These balloons have tools that take weather readings. Radios on the balloons send these measurements to weather stations.

Satellites in space gather measurements about weather across Earth, too. Some satellites stay in the same place above Earth. Other satellites circle Earth. The satellites send temperature readings and pictures of clouds to weather stations.

DID YOU KNOW?

Climate satellites take pictures of Earth's oceans, as well. These pictures let scientists trace how the currents, or patterns of water movement, in the oceans change.

Mount Washington Observatory, in New Hampshire, is a well-known weather station. In 1934, scientists measured winds of 231 miles per hour (372 km/h) there!

Working in Labs

Lots of climate scientists work in labs. These scientists often use a tool called radar to find out how much rain or snow is falling in a certain area. Radar shows the speed and direction of wet weather, too.

Climate scientists feed the measurements from radar and from other tools, such as satellites and weather stations, into fast supercomputers. The supercomputers help scientists track the present weather around the world. The scientists show the weather on maps, called synoptic charts. Climate scientists also use supercomputers to make **models** of an area's climate. These models show an area's temperature, rainfall, wind speeds, wind patterns, and other conditions.

Scientists in labs also study samples, or small amounts of something, that were gathered earlier. This scientist is studying an air sample from a weather balloon.

Learning from the Rocks

Some climate scientists study how climates change over time. One way scientists learn about past climates is by studying rocks. Climate scientists often study sedimentary rock. This rock forms when mud, sand, and small stones build up and harden into rock over a long time. Scientists learn what the climate was like when pieces of sedimentary rock formed by studying the matter that makes up the rock.

Some rocks have fossils, or the remains of living things, in them. Scientists can tell if an area's climate was cold, hot, or rainy from the kinds of plant and animal fossils they find buried there.

DID YOU KNOW?

Scientists have found snail fossils in Egypt that lead them to believe that parts of northern Africa, which are now dry deserts, were rich grasslands 130,000 years ago.

These fossilized fish show that the dry land where they were found once lay under a river, lake, or ocean.

Clues in Ice and Trees

Ice also holds clues to past climates. Climate scientists go to Greenland and Antarctica to study glaciers, or giant sheets of ice that formed long ago. Scientists drill into glaciers and remove long cores, or rods, of ice. The ash, salt, dust, and gases in ice cores tell scientists about the past's climate.

Tree rings also teach scientists about the past. Each year a tree lives, it adds a new ring to its trunk, or woody stem. Scientists drill into trees and remove cores of wood to study these rings. Thick rings mean it was warm and wet when the trees grew. Thin rings show it was cold and dry.

These climate scientists are taking ice-core samples in Antarctica. Scientists can trace how climates change over hundreds of thousands of years with ice-core samples.

Predicting Climate Change

Climate scientists use what they have learned about past climates to piece together an idea of how Earth's climate has changed over time. This allows the scientists to predict how climates might change in the future.

While Earth's climate has always changed, scientists have found that it is changing more quickly today than it did in the past. This is because people's actions are now driving climate change. Using climate models from computers, climate scientists think climate change will make temperatures rise. This could lead to more strong storms.

DID YOU KNOW?

Scientists believe that forests will have fewer trees with needles and more trees with leaves in the next 100 years. Ice sheets covering Greenland and Antarctica will get smaller and oceans will rise, too.

These scientists are studying tiny animals called coral in the waters off Florida. They learned that Earth's changing climate has already changed the coral living there.

21

An Important Job

Climate scientists help people live with Earth's changing climate. To do this important job, these scientists have to know a lot. Climate scientists spend many years studying math, computers, and science.

If you are interested in climates, you might want to try recording weather measurements every day. Write down how much of the sky is covered by clouds. Use a thermometer to read the temperature. Use a wind vane and record the wind direction. You can build a rain gauge to measure rainfall, too. Just mark inches or centimeters on the side of a clear cup. This is a great way to get your start as a climate scientist!

GLOSSARY

anemometer (a–neh–MAH–meh–tur) A tool used to measure how fast the wind is.

area (ER–ee–uh) A certain space or place.

atmosphere (AT–muh–sfeer) The gases around an object in space.

eruptions (ih–RUP–shunz) When gases, smoke, or melted rock come out of volcanoes.

future (FYOO–chur) The time that is coming.

hygrometer (hy–GRAH–meh–ter) A tool used to measure the amount of water in the air.

models (MAH–dulz) Things people make to show how something works or looks.

patterns (PA–turnz) The ways something can happen over and over again.

predict (prih–DIKT) To make a guess based on facts or knowledge.

satellites (SA–tih–lyts) Spacecraft that circle Earth.

surface (SER–fes) The outside of anything.

temperatures (TEM–pur–cherz) Measures of how hot or cold something is.

thermometers (ther–MAH–meh–terz) Tools used to measure temperature.

A
anemometer, 10
area(s), 4, 8, 14
ash, 6, 18
atmosphere, 6, 8

C
clouds, 6, 12, 22

E
Earth, 6, 8, 12

H
hygrometer, 10

M
meteorologists, 8
models, 14, 20

P
patterns, 4, 14
people, 6, 22
place(s), 4, 6, 12

R
rock(s), 6, 16

S
satellites, 12, 14

T
temperature(s), 8,
   10, 14, 20, 22
thermometer(s), 10,
   22

WEB SITES

Due to the changing nature of Internet links, PowerKids Press has developed an online list of Web sites related to the subject of this book. This site is updated regularly. Please use this link to access the list:
www.powerkidslinks.com/exsci/climate/